# SAILING IN THE OCEAN OF VERSES

## A COLLECTION OF FOURTEEN VIVIDLY WRITTEN POEMS

SCARLETT EMILY SCOTT

*"For my dearest grandfather, who has always encouraged me to do things in a uniquely different way. His memories have emboldened me to finally pen down my first book. I know he would be greatly proud of me."*

# Contents

## Contents

# Foreword

by Tisha Taneja

I have, for as long as I can remember, always wanted to write something. First, just because I read so many books that my parents thought it was a given that I'd end up writing something. They would walk in on me, hunched on my bed with a book in my lap and legs sticking out of the blanket; they'd let out a long, suffering sigh and say, "You better be planning to write something after all that reading, or else it's useless." And I would nod absently, so engrossed in the book, that I hadn't registered a single word. But as I grew up, I knew that I did want to write. I loved writing, putting my thoughts into words that allowed me to eloquently express something. When I write, I feel like I can connect to a deeper part of me. To send your words out into the world and to have people read your books, seemed, still does, like a dream I'll never quite be able to wrap my head around.

Then here comes, S. E. Scott, a great friend of mine. And she just went and put out a book. She wrote poems, chose the best of them, edited them, arranged them, and she just did it. She went out and got her book published. I may still be in awe. It's her first book, but the poems it contains, induce such meanings that you would bet this was a seasoned author.

The whole collection of Sailing in the Ocean of Verses has a whimsically beautiful feel to it. The poems are satisfying to read aloud, and the lines flow so smoothly that they take your breath away. I felt the winds as she described them and heard the sound of raindrops as I read her poem. Whether Scarlett is describing the weather or a murder, her poems are put so gracefully that I kept pausing at the lines, just so that I could reread them and admire the wordplay. I felt the innate urge to keep flipping the pages and getting lost in her words.

What higher praise could a book get than that?

# Preface

I assume you already know my name. I certainly do not have to talk about myself, give a long, detailed introduction about myself, and bore you right before you even start reading the main content. So, I will just directly start with how I came about writing this poetry book and what exhorted me to write poems.

Veraciously speaking, I did not know that I had the innate talent to write poems. Around a year back, in 2020, I lost my greatest gift, my grandfather. Naturally, all of us where grief-stricken and lost in the wonderful memories with him. I could not come to terms with the fact that my grandfather was just not physically there anymore. But somehow I learnt from my family that, brooding over what happened and that was not in our control, was a waste of time. Rather, remembering the good moments shared with him using the same time was better. Now, one fine day, I was thinking about my most lovely memories with my grandfather and decided to write it down on paper. I thought of writing them in poetic form. Once I had finished writing, I had an epiphany that I could write poems. This was the mere instance that sparked my interest in poems.

Flash back to when I was in fifth grade. We had amazing poems and extracts from novels written by the choicest of poets and authors in our English book. I always dreamt of the day when I would write poems and the generation about a hundred years from now, would get to see them in their literature textbooks. And here I am, writing my very own, first poetry book.

My daddy is great at English. It is quite hereditary, actually. I often show him my writings and he appreciates them a lot. I always share my poems with my uncle and it was a great revelation, at least for me, when I got to know that he too, writes poems. So, we appreciate each others work when he sends me his poems and when I send him mine. And this urges me to write poems. One more thing, my mother and sister, too, turned out to like my poems. They're always appreciative of them. My grandmother, she is very fond of poems. More often than not, she shares with me poems from her childhood, and this too adds to my interest in writing poems. It's a great feeling to finally be publishing my first book. Enough, now, you can start reading the book. Enjoy!

# Acknowledgements

It is a joyous feeling to have had the best set of people, who enthusiastically helped and supported me to produce this collection of poetry pages that contain vivid emotions in words. Thus, I would be obliged to thank all those who have helped and supported me, which has resulted in the publication of my first book. Firstly, to the whole of my family for always appreciating my work, reading my poems with much interest, and giving wonderful feedbacks. Then, to my eminently great friends, who have collectively cheered for me to write amazing poems each time. In particular, I thank Vaishnavi Hiremath for helping me with the title of this book and for pestering me to put my work out to the public. To, another one of my friend, Tisha Taneja for designing the back cover and writing the brilliant foreword. Also to Jofil Mary, for pushing me to the edge of the cliff, for making my first book splendid and presentable. To Ananya Ayarekar, for being greatly happy on hearing the news of my books publication and who is always ready to help in all ways possible and celebrates even the tiniest of my achievements. And to my friend, Dhwani Prasad for reading my poems and enjoying them, which encouraged me to write better poems each time.

Lastly, to all my fantastic teachers who have always been the utmost helpful when I needed them. Names go to, Mrs. Monika Solanki, for always believing in me and encouraging me to do my best; Forever grateful for your guidance and affection. Then, to

Mrs. Rajeshwari, for getting to know my interest in writing poems and appreciating it. To, Mrs. Priyanka Prakash for always being there to read my poems, being happy for me and gladly appreciating my work. Lastly, to Mrs. Neelam Ahlawat for urging me to write more poems and publish them, for the world to see. I cannot thank enough people for helping me take my first big step, so, I thank each and every person who has contributed even the slightest bit, that has yielded this poetry book.

# Idyllic Poems

# 1. Country Side Memory

*There is a fine country boy,*
*Living in a big old town.*
*But living not a happy life,*
*He often lives with a frown.*

*His heart goes back to the countryside,*
*Where the vehicles and wagons are few.*
*Where the early sun rises between the mountains,*
*And there is water on trees as drops of dew.*

*He wants to go back to the place,*
*Where there would be mountains of golden hay.*
*He remembers of how in the late afternoon,*
*Reading a book, on the heaps he would lay.*

*Later in the windy evenings,*
*He would watch the river flow.*
*He would see the different fishes,*
*Swimming merrily down below.*

*Always, the birds singing a song,*
*In the distance there are the dancing trees.*
*The country side is such a place,*
*There is calmness, joy and peace.*

*He thinks of his farm and country house,*
*Right beside the dense green wood.*
*Watching the rabbits run back and forth,*
*The grassy land, was where he stood.*

*There are butterflies flying over flowers,*
*And the yellow bees buzzing around.*
*The tulips and sweet pea blooming,*
*Blissful is, the spring time sound.*

*No more did he want to be away from home,*
*He wanted to go, where he felt blest.*
*So he started on a journey for miles and miles,*
*Back to the countryside; for the place he left.*

# 2. A Paradise Place

*It is a calm and tranquil summer day,*
*I am lost in my mind, in the thoughts that play.*
*I walk on the warm and soft sand,*
*I walk across the shore, to my mind's peaceful land.*

*I want to sing a song about all that I see,*
*Thus, I sing the song of happiness and glee.*
*The cold water, touches my feet,*
*As I look at the line, where the sun and sea meet.*

*The sun shines bright, in noon time's glow,*
*It is quiet and still and the clouds are moving slow.*
*I feel wonderful here, for emotions never lie,*
*With the glistening water, the ocean, a starlit sky.*

*I have forgotten all my sorrows, I do not worry anymore,*
*For I most enjoy the sound, of the waves hitting the shore.*
*Thou can only dream, of being on this paradise,*
*Where the sun sets on water, and a yellow morning sunrise.*

# 3. A Long Way Home

*Sometimes in the middle of an island,*
*Sometimes near a lake .*
*I was a wanderer; when not having money,*
*With a bread loaf, I could make.*

*From the places of north and south,*
*Everywhere I would roam.*
*Yet, when midnight fell,*
*I felt the need to find a home.*

*One time early morning, I woke up from sleep,*
*I had slept on the attic floor.*
*A good man had given me shelter,*
*For a night and two days more.*

*I went down and thanked the man,*
*Collected my things and coat.*
*I thought I would travel to the countryside,*
*Through the sea and on a boat.*

*I knew this was going to be ardous,*
*But I still set sail, afar.*
*I had a can of corn with me,*
*That the old man gave and a small biscuit jar.*

*Two days passed, I was glad as could be,*
*Even though I didn't have money.*
*But money never enthralled me,*
*I was happy to be on this journey.*

*During the sailing days, I slept on the boat,*
*And gazed at the night sky.*
*I loved the twinkling reflection on water,*
*And saw the dolphins passing by.*

*I thought all night about what I would do,*
*After reaching the country side.*
*Then I decided to start a farm of my own,*
*Build a home on a field, large and wide.*

*When I woke up the in the morning,*

*I saw the sea glinting like never before.*
*I looked at the beautiful day,*
*And in no time, I was on the shore.*

*I left the boat and started forward,*
*Rested a while and then got walking.*
*I crossed a bridge far ahead,*
*After a bit, saw two men talking.*

*I went up to them and asked directions,*
*They said they were going the same.*
*So we walked together to a stable nearby,*
*And rode on horses; tame.*

*We travelled for three days straight,*
*Sharing food, talks and drinks.*
*I realized there was nothing a man could not do,*
*"He can do it" if he thinks.*

*That is how I reached my home,*
*The country side, vast and green.*
*On the way I saw birds and animals,*
*And other things that had been.*

*I settled in the place I had come to,*
*I felt as if , I had forgotten sorrow.*
*I was happy, with how far I had come,*
*Cherished every bit of life; yesterday, today and morrow.*

*Now the years had gone by*
*And I had grown old.*
*I was happy with the life I had lived,*
*Through rain, summer and cold.*

*I was living a wonderful life,*
*I had built a house and farm.*
*I earned and ate my heart's full,*
*In my country side home, verdant and calm.*

# 4. A Dream of My Favorite Place

*Unable to fall asleep,*
*By my window sill, I sit.*
*Wondering about a place,*
*Somewhere, I would love to visit.*
*On the highest of the green hills,*
*There's a forest quite faraway.*
*With the fireflies it glows in the night,*
*And it shines with the sun rays, during the day.*

*The forest is filled with animals and birds,*
*And tall pine trees; grove.*
*On the ground is, soft green grass,*
*And the forest is nature's trove.*
*There is a placid lake nearby,*
*And a small cottage, for me stay.*
*The lake is quiet and still,*
*And the cottage is made of wood and hay.*

*When it is almost dark and evening time,*
*The sun sets amongst the clouds and trees.*
*The sun glows orange in the sky,*
*There blows the soothing, light breeze.*
*After dusk, and a wonderful evening,*
*It always is, a beautiful night.*
*The blue and starry sky,*
*With the white moon, a heavenly sight.*

*Then in the morning, the sun rises slowly ,*
*From beside the pellucid lake.*
*The birds start singing and the bees start buzzing,*
*What a wonderful morning they make.*
*I dream of a place of such beauty,*
*I think of it, night and day.*
*I love to see this forest in my mind,*
*This place is more enchanting than I can say.*

# Rain Poems

# 5. After the Rain

*I watch the sky slowly unfold,*
*After a rain that came untold.*
*I see, little birds and insects from around,*
*Coming out, making thier endearing sound.*
*I see raindrops on the trees and plants,*
*And damp grass along the hillside slants.*
*There isn't anything more calming,*
*Than to walk barefoot on wet grass,*
*Hear the birds chirp, and slowly let the time pass.*

*The smell of rainwater mixed with earth.*
*One of the choicest of smells that has a lot of worth.*
*I do not see its worth in currency,*
*It gives me peace, and that is what I fancy.*

*I see grasshoppers hopping in the distant fields,*
*I feel the excitement in me, that steadily builds.*
*Such an idyllic sight, I want to sit here all day long,*
*I realize, nature is the place to which I truly belong.*
*Such beautiful rains, are one of a kind,*

*It is a fresh atmosphere, where one can unwind.*
*Standing under a tree, I watch the sky slowly unfold,*
*After a lovely rain, that came untold.*

# 6. Pleasant Sounds the Droplets Make

*I love the pleasant sounds,*
*The droplets make,*
*falling on the ground.*

*The rain falls sometimes straight,*
*Sometimes slanting*
*But the pleasant sounds,*
*The droplets make*
*On the ground*
*Is forever enchanting.*

*I love the mesmerizing sounds,*
*The droplets make,*
*Falling on the ground.*

*The more I gaze at the rain,*
*With glinting eyes,*

*The more desperate I get*
*To pull my tongue out,*
*And catch droplets*
*From the rain, of every size.*

*I love the calming sounds*
*The droplets make,*
*Falling on the ground.*

*The rain falls sometimes straight,*
*Sometimes slanting,*
*But the wonderful sounds ,*
*The droplets make,*
*On the the ground,*
*Is forever enchanting.*

# Quiver of Other Wonderful Poems

# 7. The Sun's Quandary

*The sun, looked in awe at a lady*
*Her dress looking beautiful under the clear sky.*
*She had a fine floral dress on her,*
*Looking like petals of the tulips nearby.*

*Swaying with the wind so gracefully,*
*Delicate looking and yellow.*
*Beside her, were the planted tulips,*
*Sun rays touch the petals, and make them glow.*

*Now the sun, was in quite the quandary.*
*Which of the two, looked more appealing.*
*The sun shone much brighter, to look at them even better so,*
*Found them both greatly enchanting and none unappealing.*

*The lady looked bonnie with the dress,*
*That looked like petals of the tulip.*
*But the tulip seemed gorgeous too,*
*As the woman took care of the flowers root to tip.*

*Perhaps she seemed pretty, with the tulip dress she wore,*
*Appearing cheerful under the sky; blue.*
*But because she watered the tulips so well,*
*The flowers looked much charming too.*

*The lady, seems much elegant,*
*The tulip too is graceful in its essence.*
*I'm loath to believe, that only one be labelled greater, for I say,*
*None are beauteous than the other; but both are fairly different*
*in noble sense.*

# 8. Whatever Life Is

*Nothing stays forever,*
*Goes away later or now.*
*Enjoy the things when there,*
*Find joys in them somehow.*

*Problems are similar to when,*
*Dust collects on trees and flower.*
*But the good time as in, the rain when comes,*
*They wash away with the rain's shower.*

*Not everywhere is it always dark,*
*Sometime, somewhere it's still very bright.*
*But one has to keep trying hard,*
*Be patient and wait for the light.*

*The circle of life is just as such,*
*Good and bad both reside.*
*However, it depends on staying happy or sad,*
*But depending on what you decide.*

*Life again is like a road trip,*
*Go too fast, great views are missed.*
*When you slow down little, stop for a bit,*
*You know that life is truly blissed.*

# 9. The Golden Quill

*In the palace of Berteland lived,*
*A bird coloured darling yellow.*
*What thou would think as a regular bird,*
*She was special, and kept in a chamber below.*

*She was small but was beautiful too.*
*One feather in her wing stood out shining gold.*
*The bird had a secret, which was revealed one day,*
*That, through the years had remained untold.*

*The golden feather, was made into a quill,*
*It shone the sun's glow.*
*The one who held the quill, near paper,*
*His heart's deepest desires it would show.*

*People from all over the kingdom,*
*Came in hopes to try the quill.*
*Then the people asked, who should try it first,*
*The king from his throne screamed, " I will, I will! "*

*The king waited for the feather to start writing,*
*While he held the quill in his hand.*
*It went on writing, then it showed,*
*More money and power, was the king's demand.*

*Then was the turn of the peasants,*
*And the ministers, in the court.*
*All the people tried, every rich poor and pauper.*
*One by one for everyone, money and riches it wrote.*

*One last man was still left in the crowd,*
*It was now his turn to try the quill.*
*But he told the king, he hadn't come for writing,*
*He had come there only to see, from afar a hill.*

*Yet the people asked him to,*
*Have a go at his deepest desire,*
*He held the the quill, but told the king,*
*I have just enough, even though I am poor, sire!*

*The quill now wrote nothing for span of time,*

*It showed no desire at all.*
*The king gazed at the man in disbelief,*
*And so shocked were the people in the hall.*

*The poor man pleasantly smiled and said,*
*I desire neither luxury nor power.*
*I get just enough to eat every day,*
*Thus I am satisfied my life, every hour*

*The king and his people learnt a lesson that day,*
*He was rich, yet not satisfied with what he had.*
*While the man being poor still,*
*Got just enough to live, and he was happy with that.*

# 10. The Wind and the Sun

*The suns when, gets angry,*
*Throws, beams and rays of fire.*
*The wind, when in a bad mood,*
*Turns into the tempest, that one doesn't desire.*

*Verily, one can choose neither the sun nor the wind alone,*
*The sun after all, gives you warmth and shows you bright.*
*If wind, doesn't blow its soft, breeze in the heat of summer,*
*One will desiderate for the amiable wind; morn, noon and night.*

# 11. A Farmer's Joy

*A dark and cloudy day it was,*
*For the sun had taken a break.*
*The rain gods had made up their mind.*
*To give the first rain in years, as the crops were at stake.*

*Drought-like conditions, of the crops,*
*But finally the rain came on that day.*
*First droplets falling on the dusty dry saplings,*
*Was more relieving, than the people could say.*

*The dry ground now, was all wet and nice.*
*One farmer so happy, buzzing like a bee.*
*Ah, such a rain in a long, long time,*
*is good for the crops! quoth he.*

*One little boy standing in the corner,*
*Caught the eye of god, who he could not see.*
*All year long the boy had prayed, for the rain to come,*
*Today, he was ecstatic as can be.*

*As a gift from god for the little boy ,*
*The rain gave way to a beautiful rainbow.*
*The farmers saw this, it became hope to them for*
*The next crops, that they would sow.*

*The rain gave a bountiful crop that year.*
*But it came as a result of the prayers of the little boy.*
*Who won the people's heart,*
*As the rain is a farmer's joy!*

# 12. The Unexplored Ocean

*He wishes to seek what lies farther in the ocean,*
*But he is too scared, to do so.*
*Perhaps, if he doesn't gather the grit,*
*And doesn't explore, he will never know.*

*Where he is standing now,*
*Is on the trodden, soft sand.*
*He won't find what's there into the deep,*
*If he doesn't decide to leave the land.*

*Scorching heat because of the sun,*
*Blazing and much bright it shone.*
*Under it, is the vast blue water,*
*Where lies, all the danger unknown.*

*He makes up his mind and chooses,*
*To take a boat and sail from the shore.*
*But once he is in the great, colossal ocean,*
*It could be eminently perilous or more.*

*It might take him an hour or a hundred.*
*However, he will find what he wants to seek.*
*On the way he'll face the dangers and beauty,*
*He will have to fight for sustenance in the ocean; bleak.*

*By his luck or by his sapience,*
*He found an ineffably beautiful island.*
*Green prolific trees and sun rays on the leaves,*
*He held himself alive, eating fruits, much exotic and grand.*

*He did indeed hesitate for this excursion,*
*However, he chose to explore, although alone.*
*If he hadn't at all tried this adventure,*
*Of the discovery, he wouldn't have known.*

# 13. The Third Hour Murder

*A house of dark brown bricks,*
*The only house under the sky.*
*It's deep down in the forest;*
*Not a soul to be walking by.*

*But when the night had fallen,*
*Came two figures of dark colour.*
*Walking briskly and hands holding knife,*
*Scrutinizing the area, whispering to each other.*

*They don't go into the house just yet,*
*Too busy scattering dry leaves all over.*
*Making it look like an abandoned house,*
*They quietly walk to a bush and take cover.*

*A black vintage clock hanging beside the door,*
*It's half past two, the men are patient now.*

*They look at one another and signal,*
*To execute the plan, when, where and how.*

*The second floor window was warmly lit,*
*The fire burning softly in the fireplace.*
*There lay a thin man on a yellow rocking chair,*
*Blithely reading a rusty book with a intrigued look on his face.*

*It was cold, gloomy and dark outside;*
*Ate at night, yet the man was reading.*
*Fifteen minutes to three, the clock said,*
*Towards the door, the men started heading.*

*They walked up the stairway,*
*Following the warmth of the fire.*
*Looking through the keyhole of the room,*
*Caught a glimpse of a the man in night's attire.*

*They saw he had dozed off to sleep,*
*Right there, on his rocking chair.*
*An even easier situation for the men it was,*
*They thought, as they gave the room a quick stare.*

*They saw a shabby bed and an open wardrobe,*
*Sets and kits of dangerous knives.*
*They saw a dirty and bloody coat on the hanger,*
*And guns and sticks of different types.*

*The men murdered the victim,*
*As soon as the clock striked three.*
*They stole any precious objects,*
*Cleared every evidence and flee.*

*One week after, they found*
*A Newspaper upon the bookshelf.*
*They read to find that William Ferter, had been murdered a week ago,*
*Realizing, they had murdered a murderer himself*

# 14. Forgotten Memories

*Nowhere but in the middle of the ocean,*
*Here's where I stand, on an old ship.*
*Waves clashing on the rough gray rocks*
*Glistening water, adding to the gleam in my eyes.*

*I dreamt of the memories I made as a young child,*
*Could it, be near somewhere?*
*If so, it would be locked in a golden chest.*
*It must be full of magical memories from the past.*

*My dream was woken up by a boisterous storm, that swept into the ocean.*
*My ship did not drown nor was harmed,*
*But the violent water now carried the ship,*
*Far into another direction, unknown.*

*The storm was lulled, and the next day brought me ashore.*
*My eyes opened to a clear blue sky,*
*And to the golden, warm sand.*

*There in the distance, I saw a chest that lay half buried.*

❧❧❧

*I went walking to the chest, that seemed, all new and fresh still.*
*No rust had touched neither metal lock, nor the wood box.*
*I found a key, very brown and roughly broken,*
*Yet I tried it to the lock, and it opened.*

❧❧❧

*I didn't find, gold coins, jewels or loot,*
*Rather I found something much more valuable, not mundane.*
*All my best memories played above the chest I found,*
*Right in front of my surprised eyes.*

❧❧❧

*I sat there all day long looking at,*
*The great memories, from the days I was a child.*
*Sometimes a change of direction is quite good, whether by a violent storm or a row of the boat.*
*Finally, I had come to rejoice the lovely memories, forgotten and the days gone old..*

# Author Biography

" Poetry is when your feelings aren't only yours anymore and when they appeal to the reader through written words of beauty. " As quoted by Scarlett.

Scarlett Emily Scott, in short, S. E. Scott is a poetess who writes poems under a wide range of themes. She lives in Bangalore with her family and was born in 2007. Scarlett does write nature poems a lot but also pens ballard-like poems that are a little long but eloquent. She often describes a scene or tells a story in a narrative voice using poetry. She loves to travel, write and do almost everything under the sun that speaks of adventure. Being someone, who is very fond of the great outdoors and nature, she writes remarkably of beautiful scenery and poems that narrate a story, set in the enchanting cradle of nature itself. It is quite conspicuous when you read her poems.

*"Sailing in the Ocean of Verses"* is her debut book and has already elicited astounding feedback from people. She is an avid reader and has much interest in the English language. She writes poetry that speaks of what she likes, depicts very deep meanings, and takes the reader on an exciting ride of feelings. She has a fascination for rather, old English classic poets and authors. A plethora of her poems are influenced in some way or the other by many of her favorite poets and writers. Scarlett makes every effort to put on paper a better poem each time. She thinks,

" A perfect poem is one, which you adore from the bottom of your very own heart. "

# Author's Favourite

Firstly, let me make it very clear that I admire all of my writings. Yet, every poet and author has their one beloved work that always gets to shine a little more in the writer's eye. Similarly, I too have one, and it is one that is among this collection. "The Sun's Quandary", is my poem that I love most. Why you ask? You could say, because of the remarkable delineation of the poem. I believe you have already read the poem, and will be able to absorb the facts for which I favour this poem. It talks about the sun, that is awestruck at a lady, wearing a smooth flowing frock/dress that has a design featuring petals of beautiful tulips. It appears wonderful on her and she looks amazingly pretty.

Whereas, on the other hand, the sun also sees a lot of fresh glowing tulips that the same lady has planted in her probable garden or front yard. The sun, now is confused on which one, the lady with the tulip dress or the tulips themselves look better. The thing is, the lady looks beautiful only because of the design of the tulips. So, naturally, the tulips get the credit. But, the tulips themselves, look graceful and resplendent, only because the lady took such good care of them. Now, without a doubt, the credit goes to the lady. So, the poem articulately describes that both of them complement each other, and that not one alone can be chosen as the best. Each has their own points of beauty and on a different level. In the end, it is decided that , none of them can be chosen greater, as not one of them is better than the other; but both are fairly different and beautiful. The poem could be called the epitome of brevity, and that is quite apt.

No one, really is greater than the other; each has their own highlights. Everyone is fairly different. And that concludes finally, why I adore this poem. I hope you too have enjoyed this poem.

# Dear Reader

I am glad that you have read until the end. I heartfully thank you for taking the time and reading my poems. Assuming that you have enjoyed reading what I have expressed through my poetry, I can tell you that, I expect to write more poems and publish my next book that will hopefully excite you in the same way.

To connect with the author and write reviews or feedbacks, drop a mail on: scarlettemilyscott@gmail.com

9 798886 843156

Printed by Libri Plureos GmbH in Hamburg, Germany